IF PREHISTORIC WERE HERE TODAY

WERE HERE TODAY

SAVAGE PREDATORS

Thanks to the creative team:

Senior Editor: Alice Peebles
Consultant: Neil Clark
Fact checking: Kate Mitchell
Design: www.collaborate.agency

First published in Great Britain in 2016
by Hungry Tomato Ltd
PO Box 181
Edenbridge
Kent, TN8 9DP

A CIP catalogue record for this book is
available from the British Library.

ISBN 978-1-910684-76-4

Printed and bound in China

Discover more at
www.hungrytomato.com

IF PREHISTORIC BEASTS WERE HERE TODAY

SAVAGE PREDATORS

by Matthew Rake
Illustrated by Simon Mendez

HUNGRY
TOMATO™

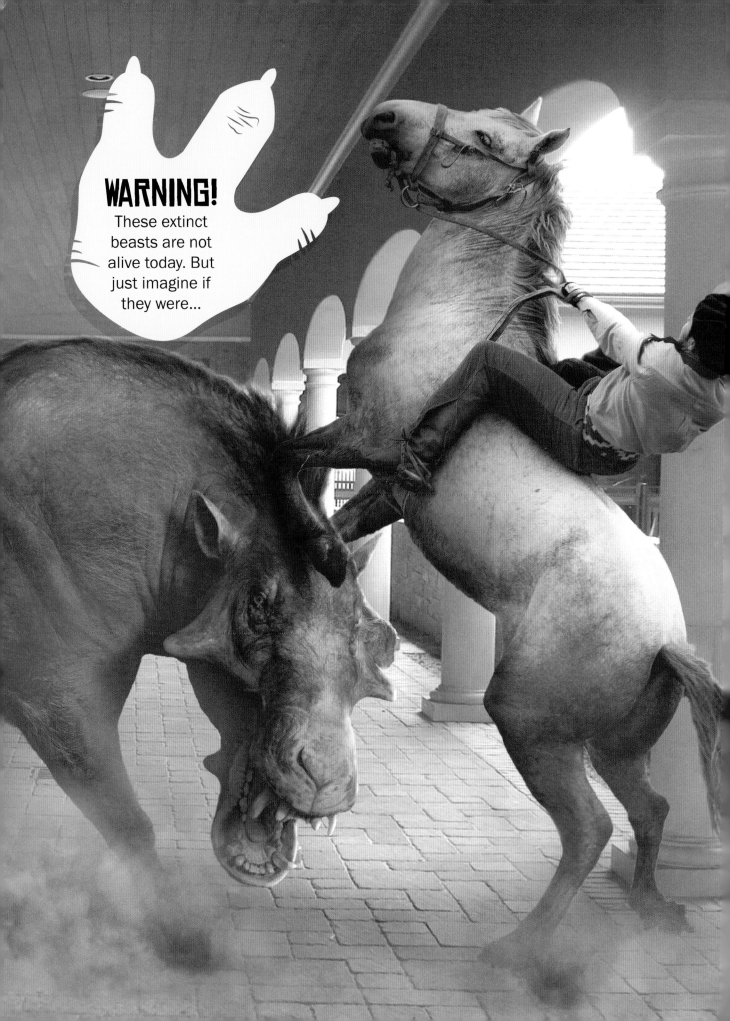

WARNING!
These extinct beasts are not alive today. But just imagine if they were...

CONTENTS

The Big, the Bad and the Ugly 6

Rocking the Boat: *Dimetrodon* 8

Ruthless Reptile: *Inostrancevia* 10

Cold-blooded Killer: *Sarcosuchus* 12

Soaring Pterosaur: *Quetzalcoatlus* 14

Walking Whale: *Ambulocetus* 16

Bone Cruncher: *Andrewsarchus* 18

Killer Pig: Entelodont 20

Terror Bird: Phorusrhacid 22

Fangtastic Feline: *Smilodon* 24

Snapping Jaws: *Hyaenodon* 26

Timeline 28

Uncovering the Past 30

Index 32

THE BIG, THE BAD AND THE UGLY

Everyone knows about the dinosaurs and how scary some of them were. But did you know there were lots of other equally savage prehistoric creatures? How about the croc that liked to dine on dinosaurs? Or the bird that stood 2.5 m (8 ft) tall and used its 46-cm (18-in) beak like a hatchet? Now can you imagine what might happen if they appeared in today's world? Well, you are about to find out...

All life started in the sea – and that's where the first animals evolved, around 550 million years ago. Some were pretty weird, such as 6-cm (2.5-in) *Opabinia* (right) with its five eyes and long grasping claw at the end of a long, hose-like arm.

Pretty soon, animals became ferocious. About 475 million years ago, there were massive predators such as sea scorpions and shelled creatures, called nautiloids, as large as crocodiles. Eventually, some sea animals evolved limbs and hauled themselves on to land. One was *Acanthostega* (below), though it probably still kept close to water.

Opabinia

Acanthostega

Reptiles were the first animals with backbones to live only on land. Some grew to enormous size, like the fearsome 'supercroc' *Sarcosuchus* (see page 12). Some evolved leathery wings and took to the skies. One of the first flying reptiles, or pterosaurs, was *Eudimorphodon* (below). **The largest was Quetzalcoatlus (see page 14), which hunted or scavenged on land.**

Eudimorphodon

Mammals started evolving at the same time as dinosaurs and pterosaurs, about 240–230 million years ago. Like the first sea creatures, they were mostly very small, but after the dinosaurs died out, **mammals grew to massive proportions.**

These big mammals were equipped with powerful jaws and muscles that made them very dangerous predators. The sabre-toothed cat, *Smilodon* (left, and page 24), which lived until 10,000 years ago, weighed up to 400 kg (880 lb) – much more than any of today's big cats. **And birds became gigantic and ferocious, too!**

Now you can **step up and meet mighty Smilodon**, along with terror birds (see page 22), killer pigs (below, and page 20) and brutal, weird-looking reptiles. Imagine them coming back to life and causing total chaos, carnage and commotion.

So if you've got the courage, read on... just be prepared for some bizarre and scary encounters between humans (or animals) and these powerful beasts.

Smilodon

Killer pigs

ROCKING THE BOAT
DIMETRODON

Er, there appears to be a rather unexpected entrant in this year's yacht race. It has a sail but it doesn't look interested in the race. In fact, it seems to be going after the sailors, not the first prize. This curious creature is *Dimetrodon* and why it had a sail on its back is a mystery. It was certainly not to help it glide across the water – although that was one of the theories when this reptile-like creature was first discovered in the 19th century. Another theory was that it might swim on its back and use the sail like a fin! Other people thought it might camouflage the animal among reeds as it waited for prey – though a better way of concealing yourself might be not having one at all!

For this capsized yachtsman, *Dimetrodon*'s sail should be the last thing on his mind – it's the teeth he should be worried about. *Dimetrodon* was one of the first animals to have serrated teeth perfect for slicing through flesh...

DIMETRODON
PRONOUNCED
Die-MEH-troe-don

LIVED
North America and Western Europe (one species), 290–270 million years ago

LENGTH
About 3 m (10 ft)

WEIGHT
225 kg (500 lb)

WARMING UP

Experts now think the sail might have controlled *Dimetrodon*'s body temperature. Just as cold-blooded reptiles need to warm up in the morning, maybe the sail helped *Dimetrodon* to soak up sunshine. Or perhaps, like the peacock's tail, it was a way of attracting mates – and the male *Dimetrodon* did have a bigger sail than the female!

EUROPEAN SPECIES

So far scientists have found 13 species of *Dimetrodon*. The first one was discovered in 1878. The latest discovery, *Dimetrodon teutonis*, found in 2001 in Germany, is the only species to have been found in Europe.

RUTHLESS REPTILE
INOSTRANCEVIA

Wolves are very territorial – they roam over many kilometres, defending their range by howling and scent-marking. But more strong-arm tactics will be necessary to tackle this impostor. It's *Inostrancevia*, which had lethal canine teeth up to 15 cm (6 in) long in its upper jaw. Its back teeth were tiny in comparison, but this didn't matter because *Inostrancevia* didn't chew its food. It simply ripped open prey and swallowed large chunks of meat. Its lower jaw was hinged so it could open its mouth very wide. One of the cubs might be swallowed whole if it really wanted to 'wolf down' its meal.

Inostrancevia lived before the age of the dinosaurs. It was a reptile but belonged to the therapsid group from which mammals evolved. Reptiles generally have sprawling limbs, but *Inostrancevia* had a more upright posture. Compared to other animals of the time, it was a good runner as its legs were long relative to the size of its body. But it is not going to outpace these wolves – they can run for 48 km (30 miles) a day. For this *Inostrancevia*, it's not a question of fight or flight. It's just fight...

INOSTRANCEVIA
PRONOUNCED
In-oh-stran-SEE-vee-ah
LIVED
Northern Russia,
260–254 million
years ago
LENGTH
up to 3.5 m (11 ft 6 in);
skull: up to 60 cm
(24 in) long

SPECIAL FEATURES

Inostrancevia is known as a gorgonopsian reptile. This order of reptiles had many mammal-like features, including different-shaped teeth, well-developed ear bones and upright legs. But they are not thought to have had fur like mammals.

COLD-BLOODED KILLER
SARCOSUCHUS

There has been major disruption on the metro system today. But finally something is emerging from the tunnel. Arriving now on platform 1 is, er... a croc. And not just any croc. This is *Sarcosuchus* – in the days of the dinosaurs, it used to lie in wait in rivers. And even the deadliest dinos needed to be extra careful. *Sarcosuchus* was the length of a bus, weighed more than an elephant and had more than 100 teeth, including bone-crushing incisors. And for protection, it was covered head to tail with scutes: hard plates covered with horn. Basically, it had its own personal suit of armour.

It was also a pretty cunning predator. Like today's crocs, *Sarcosuchus* probably waited submerged in the shallows, with its eyes just above the water. In this position, it could look around without moving its head. Unsuspecting dinosaurs that came down for a drink would end up as dinner. So a word of advice for the commuters here: 'Stand back from the platform edge – there is a *Sarcosuchus* approaching.'

SARCOSUCHUS
PRONOUNCED
Sark-oh-SUE-kuss

LIVED
Africa and
South America,
112 million years ago

LENGTH
12 m (39 ft);
skull length:
1.8 m (6 ft)

WEIGHT
8 tonnes (8.8 US tons)

TOP THAT
The biggest modern croc ever measured was Lolong, which lived in captivity in the Philippines. It was 6.17 m (20 ft 3 in) long and weighed 1.075 tonnes (1.18 US tons). *Sarcosuchus* was about eight times heavier and twice as long.

EPIC FIGHTS?
Sarcosuchus lived in what is now the Sahara in North Africa. Back then, it wasn't a desert, but a lush, tropical region with lots of rivers. *Spinosaurus*, the biggest meat-eating dinosaur ever, also lived there. It's likely the two creatures had epic fights together.

SOARING PTEROSAUR
QUETZALCOATLUS

Okay, at a watering hole, you expect giraffes. But what about the other creatures? They are *Quetzalcoatlus*, and have flown in for a quick feed. They're gobbling up the small lizards, amphibians and mammals that live around streams and lakes.

Quetzalcoatlus was a pterosaur, a type of flying reptile. Pterosaurs evolved 230 million years ago or earlier, about the same time as the dinosaurs. And just like dinosaurs, they got bigger and bigger. *Quetzalcoatlus* lived some 72–66 million years ago and was the biggest pterosaur of all. And if you think it looks big on the ground, imagine it in flight. It is the largest flying creature ever, with a wingspan as wide as a fighter jet.

One thing, however, is a little mystifying: how did this creature get in the air? Some scientists think it jumped from a cliff or used a downward slope as a runway. Others think it vaulted into the air from all fours in what they call a 'quad jump'! If so, those giraffes had better get away before they're knocked out by those giant wings…

QUETZALCOATLUS
PRONOUNCED
Kwet-ZAL-co-AT-luss

LIVED
North America,
72–66 million
years ago

LENGTH
About 10–11 m
(33–36ft)

WEIGHT
About 200–250 kg
(440–550 lb)

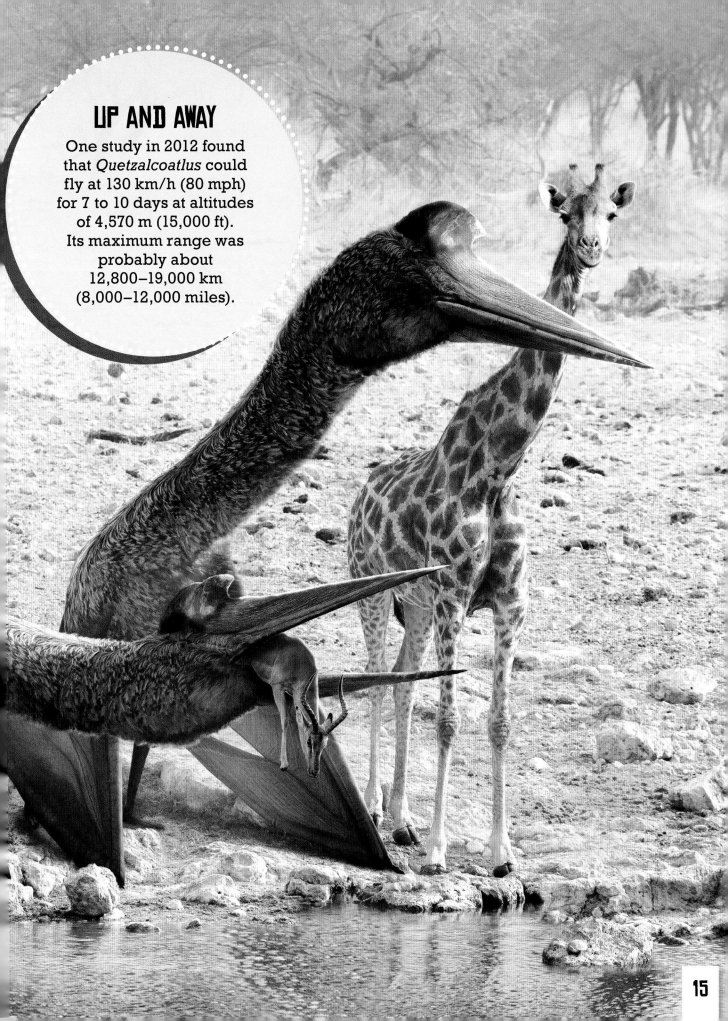

UP AND AWAY

One study in 2012 found that *Quetzalcoatlus* could fly at 130 km/h (80 mph) for 7 to 10 days at altitudes of 4,570 m (15,000 ft). Its maximum range was probably about 12,800–19,000 km (8,000–12,000 miles).

WALKING WHALE

AMBULOCETUS

Can you imagine an animal that swam like a whale but could also walk on dry land? Well, meet *Ambulocetus*. It's the big-headed animal on the right of the picture here.

On the left, a croc has just got a wildebeest by the neck – it is in the middle of killing it with its death roll. But it might have to endure a death roll of its own from *Ambulocetus*. Looks like a double dish of croc and wildebeest today for this prehistoric predator.

So how on earth did the strange-looking *Ambulocetus* come about? Around 50 million years ago, mammals were built for life on solid ground, but some started to evolve into sea creatures. Why? Probably because food was scarce on land and the sea was full of tasty treats: fish and crustaceans, such as crabs, lobsters and crayfish. One of the first to do this was *Ambulocetus*. It could walk on land but was also at home in the water – as this croc is about to find out!

GOOD VIBRATIONS

Ambulocetus probably picked up sound vibrations both in and out of the water through its lower jawbone. These sounds passed up to the inner ear. This is how modern predatory whales hear – they have no external part of the ear.

AMBULOCETUS
PRONOUNCED
Am-bew-low-SEE-tuss

LIVED
Shores of India,
50–48 million
years ago

LENGTH
About 3 m (10 ft)

WEIGHT
200–300 kg
(440–660 lb)

SPEEDY SWIMMER

Ambulocetus swam by arching its spine and pushing its lower body up and down in the water, like an otter or a whale. Powerful kicks with its back legs, which probably had webbed toes, gave the animal extra speed.

BONE CRUNCHER
ANDREWSARCHUS

In Asia, the tiger is the apex predator. This means no other animal preys on it. Big tigers can measure 3 m (10 ft) and have skulls 35 cm (13 in) long. Well, here the tiger has more than met its match – it's the monster *Andrewsarchus*.

Scientists have only ever found one skull of *Andrewsarchus*, but it is much more than double the length of a tiger's. The size of the body is anyone's guess – but if it were in the same proportion as a tiger, it would be more than 8 m (26 ft) long! Scientists don't think it would have reached these lengths – but they are pretty sure it was the largest carnivorous land mammal ever. The size of the cheekbones tell us the jaws would have had tremendously powerful muscles. These muscles, together with its huge canines, would have been perfect for delivering a fatal bite to the skull of another animal.

So, although they say don't catch a tiger by the tail, this *Andrewsarchus* shouldn't be too worried. After all, he is the apex predator here.

ANDREWSARCHUS
PRONOUNCED
Ann-droo-SAR-kuss

LIVED
Central Asia,
48–41 million
years ago

SKULL LENGTH
83 cm (32 in);
width 56 cm (22 in)

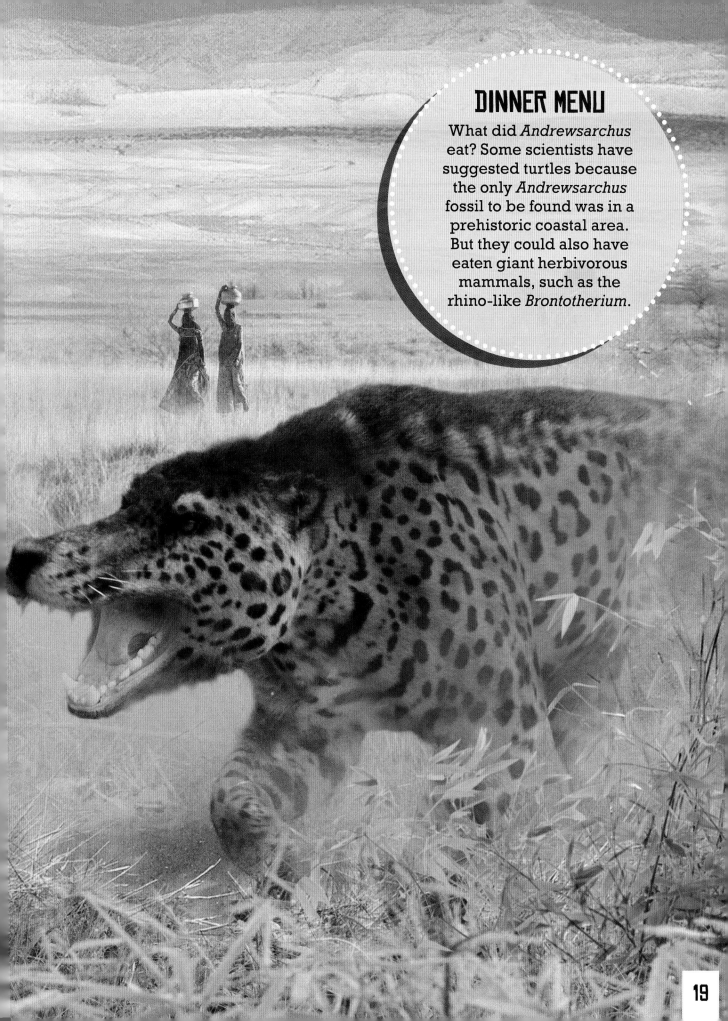

DINNER MENU

What did *Andrewsarchus* eat? Some scientists have suggested turtles because the only *Andrewsarchus* fossil to be found was in a prehistoric coastal area. But they could also have eaten giant herbivorous mammals, such as the rhino-like *Brontotherium*.

KILLER PIG
ENTELODONT

You've heard of foxes raiding a chicken shed and dogs chasing sheep in fields. But a pig terrorizing a farm? That couldn't happen. Oh yes it could, if the pig in question is an entelodont. They certainly want more than a few roots and grains on their dinner menu.

Entelodonts are often simply referred to as 'killer pigs'. And here's why. They were massive creatures, at least twice the size of today's pigs. Their huge skulls had jaws and muscles designed for bone crushing. Fossils of primitive rhinos and camels have been found with wounds that were made by entelodonts.

They would even attack their fellow entelodonts. Many entelodont skulls have severe gashes up to 2 cm (0.8 in) deep, which can only have been inflicted by other killer pigs. From studying these wounds, scientists can tell it was common for one pig to have its rival's head entirely in its mouth!

So the rancher here should get out of that barn as quickly as possible.
And if the entelodont wants to stay the night, let it!

ENTELODONT
PRONOUNCED
en-TELL-oh-dont
LIVED
North America, Europe and Asia, 37–16 million years ago
LENGTH
Up to 3.5 m (11 ft)
WEIGHT
About 420 kg (930 lb)

BIG HEAD
Daeodon was one of the largest entelodonts. It lived about 20 million years ago, and its skull was about 90 cm (3 ft) long – that's slightly bigger than a standard oil drum!

TERROR BIRD
PHORUSRHACID

The 2:30 at Ascot has an unexpected entrant. Scientists call it a 'phorusrhacid' but, as that is quite hard to pronounce, it's often called a 'terror bird'. And you can see why. With a massive head, long, powerful legs and fearsome talons, the terror bird was a bit like a smaller version of *T. rex*. So you can be sure it has not come along for the ride – it's here for the riders! And it's odds on that it will get one.

How do we know terror birds were ferocious meat-eaters? One important clue is that their beaks curved downwards into a hook-like tip. Every living bird of prey has a beak like this for tearing off flesh – so it's a clear sign that terror birds also had a taste for meat. Indeed, the terror birds' hooks were so big that scientists think they were used to strike down repeatedly on prey with quick stabbing motions. The beak could be up to 46 cm (18 in) long and some birds grew 2.5–3 m (8–10 ft) tall – so it would be a bit like someone standing over you, hitting you with a hatchet!

PHORUSRHACID
PRONOUNCED
FOR-uss-RAY-kid

LIVED
South and
North America,
60–2 million
years ago

HEIGHT
Up to about 3 m (10 ft)

WEIGHT
Up to 250 kg (550 lb)

UP TO SPEED

If you think the bird here would not keep up with the horses, think again. The fastest racehorse ran at 70.76 km/h (44 mph). Some scientists estimate that *Mesembriornis*, a 1.5-m (5-ft) terror bird, galloped along at 97 km/h (60 mph).

FANGTASTIC FELINE
SMILODON

We all know about the ferocity of today's lions, tigers and leopards. Well, they are pussycats compared to the sabre-toothed cats. These prehistoric predators were generally bigger and more powerfully built – and the largest of all was *Smilodon*. It had massively powerful front legs and fangtastic canines: they were 20 cm (8 in) long and serrated on both edges.

Smilodon lived in North and South America and hunted bison and camel, and maybe even baby mammoth and giant sloth. None of these animals survive in the wild there today – except a very few wild bison. So these *Smilodon* have found other prey: a bear.

How did *Smilodon* capture its prey? There was probably no running involved. *Smilodon* was heavily built and had a very short tail, which meant its balance and agility would have been poor, unlike most of today's big cats'. So scientists think *Smilodon* had to be more cunning – it probably pounced on prey from trees or rocks. Then it would sink its canines into its victim's neck and wait until the wounded animal bled to death.

SMILODON

PRONOUNCED
SMY-loh-don

LIVED
North and South America,
2 million–10,000 years
ago

LENGTH
1.8 m (6 ft)

WEIGHT
Up to 400 kg (880 lb)

COME TOGETHER

Scientists believe that *Smilodon* lived in packs. Why? Because fossils often show they had leg fractures that had healed. The only way they could have survived such injuries was if other members of a pack had brought them food.

SNAPPING JAWS
HYAENODON

Fancy a nice relaxing day at the beach? A spot of sunbathing, swimming and – er... escaping from a *Hyaenodon*. This creature was one of the first big carnivorous mammals. It had massive jaws supported by extra muscles in its neck – and it used them to crush animal skulls. We know this because a fossil of an early type of cat called *Dinictis* has holes in its skull that match the tooth pattern of *Hyaenodon*. What's more, fossilized *Hyaenodon* poo contains pieces of animal skull.

Hyaenodon did not rely just on crushing animals in its jaws. It also had slicing teeth at the back of those jaws. As the animal grew older, the slicing teeth would grind against each other, keeping them sharp. As a result, *Hyaenodon* could eat smaller pieces rather than gulping down large chunks, which would have helped with digestion. To avoid being chewed up into very small pieces, these beachgoers need to get up that lifeguard tower. It's a very appropriately named tower, if you think about it.

HYAENODON
PRONOUNCED
Hi-EE-noh-don
LIVED
Plains of
North America,
Europe, Asia
and Africa,
40–20 million
years ago
LENGTH
Just over 3 m (10 ft)
(the largest species,
Hyaenodon gigas)

NO
DOGS

Why did *Hyaenodon* die out? It might have had more competition from 'bear dogs', such as *Amphicyon*. These were as lethal as *Hyaenodon* but probably faster, so they were more able to catch scurrying herbivores.

TIMELINE

DIMETRODON

Named after the Greek for 'two measures of teeth'

Dimetrodons had incisors for gripping; stabbing canines; curved rear teeth for shearing flesh; and teeth in the roof of the mouth to pin down prey.

SARCOSUCHUS

Named after the Greek for 'flesh crocodile'

Sarcosuchus' long snout had a bowl-shaped ending called a 'bulla'. Scientists are not sure what it was for. It may have helped the croc to smell or allowed it to make calls to fellow *Sarcosuchus*.

QUETZALCOATLUS

Named after the Aztec flying serpent god, Quetzalcoatl

Most scientists think *Quetzalcoatlus* ate small animals on land, as a modern stork does. But others think it scavenged dead carcasses like a vulture, or skimmed up fish in its metre-long beak like a seabird.

INOSTRANCEVIA

Named after Russian geologist Alexandr Inostrantzev

The herbivore *Scutosaurus* was probably one of *Inostrancevia's* main meals. It was massively built and heavily armoured, but could not have outrun *Inostrancevia*.

PHORUSRHACID

Named after the Greek for 'bearing wrinkles or scars'

The lands of North and South America joined about 3 million years ago, and at least one species of terror bird, the *Titanis*, migrated to North America. Its remains have been found in Texas and Florida.

HYAENODON

Named after the Greek for 'hyena tooth'

Hyaenodon microdon, the smallest species of *Hyaenodon*, was not a massive wolf-sized creature – it was only about the size of a house cat, around 40–50 cm (16–20 in) long.

ANDREWSARCHUS

Named after naturalist Roy Chapman Andrews and the Greek, *archos*, for ruler

Andrewsarchus is widely considered to be the largest carnivorous land mammal ever. Today's largest is the polar bear.

SMILODON

Named after the Greek for 'knife/sabre tooth'

Sabre-toothed cats evolved from the Carnivora group of mammals about 42 million years ago. Their acute senses made them excellent hunters. *Smilodon* was one of the last sabre-toothed cats.

AMBULOCETUS

Named after the Latin *ambulare* (to walk) and *cetus* (whale)

Chemical analysis of *Ambulocetus'* teeth shows it lived in fresh and salt water. Maybe it lived in river estuaries where fresh water meets the sea – or it went anywhere to find a meal.

ENTELODONT

Named after the Greek for 'perfect tooth'

Entelodonts were probably omnivores and also apex predators in North America, Europe and Asia. *Andrewsarchus* was closely related to Entelodonts.

UNCOVERING THE PAST

Scientists reconstruct prehistoric beasts from their fossilized body parts, which helps them understand how the animals lived. One of the best-known dinosaur finds is, of course, the top predator *Tyrannosaurus rex* (right) – and one of the few complete skeletons of *T. rex* is in the American Museum of Natural History in New York City.

The displays in museums are not made from real fossil bones. These are fragile and precious, and must be carefully stored away. Instead, museum staff make lightweight replicas of fossils, and use these to construct skeletons, often covering them with synthetic skin, scales or fur (above).

'Mythical' fossils

Palaeontology, or the study of fossils, has come far since early times. There are, however, people who link tales about mythical creatures such as the griffin (a mixture of lion and eagle) to the discovery of dinosaur fossils. There is little evidence for this, but it is true that early fossil finds seemed very puzzling. In 1676 a British professor called Robert Plot was given a fossil of an unusually large thigh bone. When describing it, he said it must have come from a giant race of humans! In fact, it was from a *Megalosaurus* dinosaur...

Reconstructing skeletons

When scientists are exceptionally lucky, they find complete skeletons of animals to work from. But usually there are missing bones.The bones may have broken up while the animal was being buried. Sometimes, a predator ate some bones of the animal it killed!

However, scientists can remake the whole animal by comparing its skeleton with other skeletons of the same animal. They often know where the muscles were positioned, too, because the bones sometimes have scars where the muscles were attached. Once they have an idea of the size of the muscles, they can estimate the animal's weight.

What the skin was like is a different matter. Occasionally, when an animal is buried in fine soil that hardens quickly, it is preserved – but usually it isn't! So scientists often disagree about the skin of prehistoric animals – arguing over its colour and texture, and whether it had fur or feathers.

INDEX

A
Ambulocetus 16–17, 29
Amphicyon 27
Andrewsarchus 18–19, 29

C
crocodiles 12–13, 28

D
Dimetrodon 8–9, 28
dinosaurs 7, 12, 14, 30
fossils 30–31

E
entelodonts 20–21, 29

F
fossils 19-20, 24, 26
    30–31

H
Hyaenodon 26–27, 29

I
Inostrancevia 10–11, 28

K
killer pigs 20–21, 29

M
mammals 7
    Ambulocetus 16–17, 29
    Amphicyon 27
    Andrewsarchus 18–19,
    29
    entelodonts 20–21, 29
    Hyaenodon 26–27, 29
    Smilodon 24–25, 29

P
phorusrhacids 22–23, 28
pterosaurs 6, 14–15
    Quetzalcoatlus 14–15,
    28

Q
Quetzalcoatlus 14–15, 28

R
reptiles 6, 14
    Inostrancevia 10–11,
    28
    Sarcosuchus 12–13,
    28

S
sabre-toothed tigers
    24–25, 29
Sarcosuchus 12–13, 28
sea animals 6, 16
skeletons 30–31
Smilodon 24–25, 29

T
terror birds 22–23, 28
timeline 28–29
Tyrannosaurus rex 30

The Author
Matthew Rake lives in London, UK, and has worked in publishing for more than 20 years. He has written on a wide variety of topics for adults as well as children, including science, sport and the arts.

The Illustrator
Award-winning illustrator Simon Mendez combines his love of nature and drawing by working as an illustrator with a focus on scientific and natural subjects. He paints on a wide variety of themes but mainly concentrates on portraits and animal subjects. He lives in the United Kingdom.